From Rubbish to Riches

Plastic

Daniel Nunn

Raintree

www.raintreepublishers.co.uk
Visit our website to find out
more information about
Raintree books.

To order:
☏ Phone 0845 6044371
🖷 Fax +44 (0) 1865 312263
✉ Email myorders@raintreepublishers.co.uk

Customers from outside the UK please telephone +44 1865 312262

Raintree is an imprint of Capstone Global Library
Limited, a company incorporated in England and
Wales having its registered office at 7 Pilgrim Street,
London, EC4V 6LB – Registered company number:
6695582

Text © Capstone Global Library Limited 2012
First published in hardback in 2012
First published in paperback in 2013
The moral rights of the proprietor have been
asserted.

Edited by Rebecca Rissman, Daniel Nunn, and
Sian Smith
Designed by Joanna Hinton-Malivoire
Picture research by Tracy Cummins
Originated by Capstone Global Library Ltd
Printed and bound in China by South China
Printing Company Ltd

ISBN 978 1 406 22676 8 (hardback)
15 14 13 12 11
10 9 8 7 6 5 4 3 2 1

ISBN 978 1 406 22683 6 (paperback)
16 15 14 13 12
10 9 8 7 6 5 4 3 2 1

British Library Cataloguing in Publication Data
Nunn, Daniel. Plastic. – (From rubbish to riches)
1. Plastics craft 2. Plastics–Recycling- 3. Trash art
4. Refuse and refuse disposal. 5. Salvage
745.5'72-dc22
A full catalogue record for this book is available
from the British Library.

Acknowledgements
We would like to thank the following for permission
to reproduce photographs: Alamy p. 22a (©
PhotoStock-Israel); Corbis pp. 9, 23b (© BRIAN
SNYDER/Reuters); Heinemann Raintree pp. 4, 22c,
23e (David Rigg), 5, 6, 8, 10, 11, 12, 13, 14, 15, 16, 17,
18, 19, 20, 21, 23f (Karon Dubke); istockphoto pp. 7
(© westphalia), 22b (© subjug); Shutterstock pp.
23a (© GJS), 23c (© homydesign), 23d (© Alaettin
YILDIRIM), 23f (© Losevsky Pavel).

Cover photograph of artwork made from plastic
bags reproduced with permission of Photolibrary
(Heiner Heine). Cover inset image of plastic bags
reproduced with permission of istockphoto
(© NoDerog). Back cover photographs of a piggy
bank and a parachute reproduced with permission
of Heinemann Raintree (Karon Dubke).

Every effort has been made to contact copyright
holders of material reproduced in this book. Any
omissions will be rectified in subsequent printings if
notice is given to the publisher.

Contents

Some words are shown in bold, **like this**. You can find them in the glossary on page 23.

What is plastic?

Plastic is a man-made **material**. It can be made into lots of different shapes.

Plastic is often used in **packaging**.

When you buy food or drink from a shop, it often comes in a plastic **container**.

Water bottles, yoghurt pots, and margarine tubs are all made of plastic.

What happens when you throw plastic away?

Plastic is very useful.

But when you have finished with it, do you throw it away?

If you throw plastic away it will end up at a rubbish tip.

It will be buried in the ground and may stay there for a very long time.

What is recycling?

It is much better to **recycle** plastic than to throw it away.

Separate plastic things from your other rubbish and put them in a recycling bin.

The plastic things will be collected and taken to a **factory**.

Then the plastic will be made into something new.

How can I reuse old plastic?

You can also use old plastic to make your own new things.

When you have finished with a plastic bag, bottle, or **container**, put it away somewhere instead of throwing it away.

Soon you will have lots of plastic waiting to be reused.

You are ready to turn your rubbish into riches!

What can I make with plastic bottles?

Plastic bottles are used to hold **liquids** like milk or cola.

But you can use them to make fun piggy banks.

You can also use them to make some spooky lanterns.

It is easy to light them up using battery-powered candles.

What can I make with plastic containers?

Old yoghurt pots make perfect plant pots for herbs.

Plant a different herb in each pot, and remember to make them look nice!

You can use an ice cream tub to make a beautiful gift basket for someone special.

What will you put in yours?

What can I make with plastic bags?

Plastic bags can be used to make all sorts of things.

They can be knitted into bags and purses.

You can also use them to make parachutes for your toys.

But remember, you must NEVER put plastic bags over your head.

Make your own yoghurt-pot animals

You can use old yoghurt pots to make your own fun animals.

You will need some empty yoghurt pots, pieces of **felt** in different colours, googly eyes, scissors, and some glue.

First, cut a large piece of felt to glue around the yoghurt pot.

You could use white for a rabbit, red for a ladybird, or black pieces for a cow.

Next, cut some ears, a nose, and a mouth and glue them on to your animal.

Finally, remember to glue on your animal's eyes!

You have now finished making your first yoghurt-pot animal.

Now it's time to make it some friends!

Recycling quiz

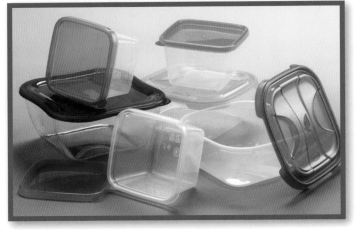

One of these things is made from **recycled** plastic. Can you guess which one? (Answer on page 24.)

Glossary

 **container** object used to put things in

 **factory** building where something is made

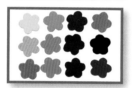 **felt** type of cloth, often used in crafts

 **liquid** substance that can flow, like water or oil

 **material** what something is made of

 **packaging** box or wrapping that something comes in

 **recycle** break down a material and use it again to make something new

Find out more

Ask an adult to help you make fun things with plastic using the websites below.

Piggy bank: **www.freekidscrafts.com/index. php?option=com_events&task=view_detail&agid=599**

Toy parachutes: **familyfun.go.com/playtime/plastic-bag-paratrooper-708602/**

You can find other ideas at: **enchantedlearning.com/crafts/straws/**

Answer to question on page 22
The clothes are made from recycled plastic.

Index